# Contents

Any words appearing in bold, **like this**, are explained in the Glossary.

About the experiments and demonstrations

In each chapter of this book you will find a section called 'Science Answers'. This describes an experiment or demonstration that you can try yourself. There are some simple safety rules to follow when doing an experiment:

- Ask and adult to help with any cutting using a sharp knife.
- Mains electricity is dangerous. Never, ever try to experiment with it
- Do not use any of your experimental materials near a mains electrical socket.

Materials you will use

Most of the experiments and demonstrations in this book can be done with objects that you can find in your own home. A few will need items that you can buy from a hardware shop. You will also need paper and pencil to record your results.

What is sound?

Have you ever experienced complete silence? You probably haven't. Even in the quietest bedroom at night you will hear the faint **sound** of distant traffic, or the rustling of trees, or the sound of the wind, or the rustling of your clothes as you move.

There is always sound around us because there is always something moving nearby – and whenever anything moves, it produces some sound, even if the sound is very faint. The reason is that sound is itself a special sort of movement – of the air, of the solid material of a wall, or of water.

Making sound

Sound is not always something that we hear coming from somewhere else. We can make sounds ourselves. When we talk we put together sounds that other people can hear and understand. **Music** consists of sounds put together to sound pleasant or exciting to the listener. Radios and television **loudspeakers** use electricity to create sounds. You will find out about how we hear and create sounds in this book.

Hushing things up

Our ears can detect even very faint sounds – like someone whispering a secret. It is hard to block sound out so that we cannot hear it. Even if we cover our ears up, some sound travels through our body and head. It reaches the insides of our ears, and may be heard – though it may be very faint and unclear.

SCIENCE ANSWERS

Sound

FROM WHISPER TO ROCK BAND

Heinemann
LIBRARY

www.heinemann.co.uk/library
Visit our website to find out more information about **Heinemann Library** books.

To order:
☎ Phone 44 (0) 1865 888066
▤ Send a fax to 44 (0) 1865 314091
▢ Visit the Heinemann Bookshop at www.heinemann.co.uk/library to browse our catalogue and order online.

First published in Great Britain by
Heinemann Library, Halley Court,
Jordan Hill, Oxford OX2 8EJ,
part of Harcourt Education.

Heinemann is a registered trademark of
Harcourt Education Ltd.

Editorial: Sarah Eason and Georga Godwin
Design: Jo Hinton-Malivoire and
  Tinstar Design Ltd (www.tinstar.co.uk)
Illustrations: Jeff Edwards
Picture Research: Rosie Garai
  and Liz Eddison
Production: Viv Hichens

Originated by Ambassador Litho Ltd
Printed and bound in China by WKT

ISBN 0 431 17495 4 (hardback)
07 06 05 04 03
10 9 8 7 6 5 4 3 2 1

ISBN 0 431 17503 9 (paperback)
08 07 06 05 04
10 9 8 7 6 5 4 3 2 1

**British Library Cataloguing
in Publication Data**
Cooper, Christopher
Sound. – (Science Answers)
534
A full catalogue record for this book is
available from the British Library.

Acknowledgements
The Publishers would like to thank the
following for permission to reproduce
photographs: Corbis/Bettmann **p. 28**;
Corbis/Joe McDonald **p. 24**; Corbis/Mark
Thiessen **p. 15**; Corbis/Michael Yamashita
p. 5; Corbis/Patrick Ward **p. 20**;
Corbis/Paul Hardy **p. 14**; Corbis/Rich
Meyer **p. 4**; Corbis/Steve Kaufman **p. 12**;
Getty Images **p. 26**; Getty Images/Barros &
Barros **p. 16**; Getty Images/Steve Bronstein
p. 9; Getty Images/Wilfred Krecichwost
p. 17; Hulton Archive **p. 29**; Photodisc
pp. 6, 11, 18; Trevor Clifford **pp. 7, 13,
19, 22, 25, 27**.

Cover photograph of the boy playing the
trumpet reproduced with permission
of Photodisc.

The Publishers would like to thank
Robert Snedden and Barbara Katz for
their assistance with the preparation of
this book.

Every effort has been made to contact
copyright holders of any material
reproduced in this book. Any omissions
will be rectified in subsequent printings
if notice is given to the Publishers.

What is noise?

'**Noise**' can be almost any sort of sound, but the word is especially applied to unwanted or unpleasant sounds, or sounds that are not clearly speech or music. The sounds of traffic and construction work in the city are noise. The louder they are, the worse the noise. But even your favourite music can be noise if it is distracting you during, say, an examination. And a sound counts as noise if it is so loud that it becomes painful to hear, or even damages your sense of hearing.

How are sounds made?

Air is all around us. We cannot see it, but we feel it when we feel a breeze or the wind. Breezes and winds are the air moving. Air is made up of huge numbers of tiny particles, called **molecules**. When an object **vibrates**, or moves back and forth quickly, the air molecules around it also vibrate. Each molecule bumps into its neighbours and makes them vibrate. The vibrations spread. When air molecules in our ears start vibrating, we hear **sounds**.

All sorts of sharp movements make air molecules vibrate and so create sounds. When you burst a paper bag, or strike two pieces of wood together, or plunge your hand into water, the sudden sharp movements disturb the air, making vibrations that spread outwards like the ripples in the water. Molecules in solids and liquids can also vibrate, so sounds can also travel through these materials.

Can anyone hear you in space?

Sound needs something to travel through – air, water, the walls of a building. Sound can travel through water even better than it can travel through air. Sound cannot travel through a vacuum. A vacuum is empty space that does not have any air molecules in it. Sound cannot reach us from the Moon, Sun or any other heavenly body because the space between them and us is a vacuum.

EXPERIMENT: How does a musical instrument make sound?

HYPOTHESIS:
Bells, guitar strings and drums vibrate to create sounds.

EQUIPMENT:
Door-chime tubes or other type of bell, a guitar or other stringed instrument, a tambourine or small drum.

EXPERIMENT STEPS:
1 Strike one of the tubes of the door chimes and note how long the note lasts. Then gently touch it with one finger while it is still making a sound. Do you feel anything?
2 Pluck or strum the guitar string. Look at it closely. What do you see? Now touch it gently with one finger, as you did with the chime. Does the sound change? How? Why?
3 Drop grains of rice or sugar on the drum or tambourine. See how they dance about as the instrument is struck.
4 Write down what you saw.

CONCLUSION:
These musical instruments vibrate when they are played. You can see and feel the vibration, and you can hear the sound made. The vibrations can be strong enough to make small objects such as grains of rice or sugar jump about.

How does sound travel?

The **vibrations** in the air that we hear as **sounds** form waves. To understand what sound waves are, they can be compared with waves or ripples on the surface of water.

A ripple spreading from the middle of a pond is a disturbance in the water. Water does not spread outwards with the ripples. A cork in the water is not carried to the edge of the pond – it moves up and down and backwards and forwards. This shows the movement of the water. Each particle of water near the surface goes up and down and backwards and forwards, in a circle. It jostles its neighbours and these jostle their neighbours, and so the movement is passed on.

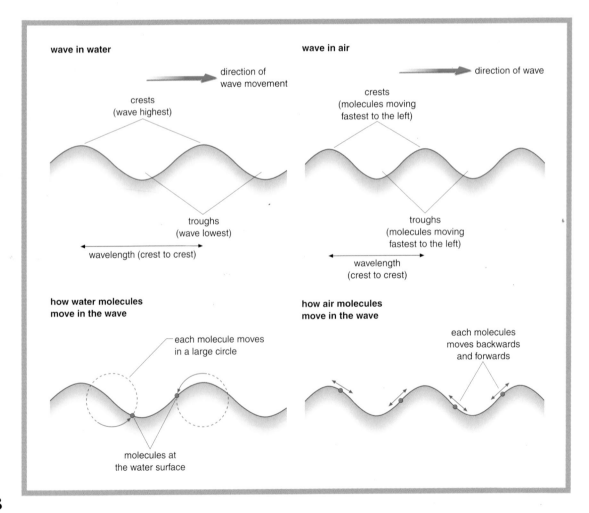

wave in water

direction of
wave movement

crests
(wave highest)

troughs
(wave lowest)

wavelength (crest to crest)

wave in air

direction of wave

crests
(molecules moving
fastest to the left)

troughs
(molecules moving
fastest to the left)

wavelength
(crest to crest)

how water molecules
move in the wave

each molecule moves
in a large circle

molecules at
the water surface

how air molecules
move in the wave

each molecules
moves backwards
and forwards

What makes a sound loud?

In a sound wave, particles of air jostle each other. The particles are **molecules** – small groups of **atoms**. The molecules move backwards and forwards. The distance by which a molecule moves backwards and forwards is called the **amplitude** of its motion.

The farther the molecules move back and forth, the faster they move, and the louder the sound is. This is because the molecules have a bigger effect on our ears if they move fast. But the distances the molecules move are always extremely small. We can hear sound waves in which the molecules move only a ten-millionth of a centimetre.

The sound of breaking glass

Sometimes sound waves can do damage, even when the sound is not very loud. Sound waves hitting this glass make it vibrate. The glass tends to vibrate at a certain number of vibrations per second. If exactly the same number of sound waves strikes the glass in each second, their effects will add together. They will make the glass vibrate so strongly that it might shatter. For example, a singer could break a glass by singing just the right note.

What is wavelength?

In a wave in water, the distance from one wave crest (the highest part) to the next is called the **wavelength**. It is also the distance from one trough (deepest part) of the wave to the next. In ocean waves the wavelength can be tens of metres. In ripples in a bath, it can be a centimetre or less.

In sound waves the air molecules move backwards and forwards, not up and down. Strictly speaking, the sound waves do not have crests and troughs. But we can call the places where air molecules are most compressed the 'crests' of the sound waves. And we can call the places where the molecules are least compressed the 'troughs'. The wavelength of the sound wave is the distance from one crest to the next, or one trough to the next. In different sorts of sound waves these wavelengths range from about 25 metres to about 20 millimetres.

What is frequency?

The rate at which waves pass a fixed point is called the **frequency** of the waves. If you watch the ocean from the end of a pier, you can count the waves that pass. Typically there might be about one every three seconds. Sound waves that human beings can hear have much higher frequencies than this, ranging from about 20 waves passing per second to about 20,000. Scientists say that the frequency of sound ranges from 20 **hertz** to 20,000 hertz.

How fast can sound go?

Sound waves move at different speeds in different materials. This is because molecules can be closer together or farther apart in different substances. In solids, the molecules are close together. In liquids, they are farther apart. They are farthest apart in gases. The closer together the molecules are, the easier it is for a vibrating molecule to disturb the molecule next to it. This makes it easier for the sound to move.

How fast do sound waves move?

Sound waves travel through air at about 340 metres per second. This is much faster than waves and ripples travel across the surface of a lake or the sea. Light travels much faster than sound, at about 300 million metres per second.

During a thunderstorm, you see the lightning before you hear the thunder. They happen at the same time but the thunder takes longer to reach your ears.

When a ship fires a gun at sea, a double bang can often be heard. The first bang is the sound that has travelled through the water. The second is the sound that has travelled more slowly through the air. The speed of sound in water is about 1500 metres per second. In air it is only 340 metres per second.

How does sonar work?

Submarines and ships use **sonar** to find the positions of objects underwater.

Sonar equipment fires pulses of high-frequency sound waves that travel through the water. They are reflected, or bounce back, from objects such as the sea bottom or shoals of fish. The sonar measures the time taken for the reflected sound pulses to return and calculates the distance of the object.

EXPERIMENT: How does sound travel?

HYPOTHESIS:
Sound consists of moving air molecules, which bump into other air molecules, moving the sound along.

EQUIPMENT:
An empty can, plastic food wrap, a little sugar, a tin tray, a wooden spoon.

EXPERIMENT STEPS:
1 Stretch the food wrap over the open end of the can and make sure it forms a tight surface, like a drum-skin.
2 Sprinkle a few grains of sugar on the plastic.
3 Hold the tin tray close to the can, but not touching it, and beat the tray very hard with the spoon while you watch the sugar grains closely. What do you see? Do you know why this happens?

4 Write down what you saw.

CONCLUSION:
The sugar grains moved and bounced around. Since the only thing that happened was that a loud sound was made nearby, the sound must have made the grains move. The air near the sugar must have moved, and the moving air moved the sugar grains.

How do we change sounds?

Sounds are not only loud or soft – they are also high or low. The voices of children are high, and those of adults are lower. The chirrup of a songbird and the jingling of sleigh-bells are high; the roar of a lion and the tolling of a church bell are lower. **Pitch** is the word we use to describe how low or high a sound is.

Why does the note of the siren change?

The pitch, or frequency, of a sound seems to alter if the number of sound waves hitting our ears alters. You may have noticed this if you have heard a police car, fire engine or ambulance driving past while sounding its **siren**. When the vehicle is coming towards you, each sound wave has a slightly shorter distance to travel to reach you than the wave before did. The time between one wave arriving and the one after it arriving is less than when the vehicle is stationary. The siren sounds higher-pitched.

When the vehicle is moving away from you, each wave takes longer to reach you than the one before did. The frequency seems reduced and the pitch seems lowered.

What makes sounds high or low?

'High' sounds have high **frequencies** – many sound waves go past per second. 'Low' sounds have low frequencies – few waves go by per second. You can hear this for yourself. If you drag a stick along railings, the separate banging sounds merge into one sound. If you do it fast, you will hear a higher **note** than when you do it slowly. The more frequently the bangs strike your ears, the higher the note that you hear. In a similar way, the more frequently that individual sound waves strike your ears, the higher the sound you hear.

Bigger means lower

These bells sound a range of notes. The biggest bells have the lowest pitch, and the smallest bells have the highest.

How do musical instruments work?

Musical instruments are designed to produce sounds that are loud, like a drum, or long-lasting, like the note of a violin. Usually those sounds also have a definite, but easily controlled, pitch.

One large 'family' of musical instruments has strings. Guitars, harps, pianos and violins have strings or wires that **vibrate** after being plucked, struck or stroked. While the string vibrates it sends out sound waves. A string sounds higher if it is thinner, shorter or more tightly stretched.

How do we get a sound by blowing?

Another large family of musical instruments are the wind instruments. All of these use moving air to make sound.

An instrument such as a flute or trumpet contains a column of air. Blowing into it or across the end of it sets the air inside it vibrating.

How do you change the pitch of a string?

A guitar has six stretched strings of different thicknesses. They are either plucked or struck. The guitarist gets different notes not only by selecting different strings but also by altering the length of each string. The player can press each string down with their fingers at different positions along the neck of the guitar. This creates different lengths of string that the player can pluck or strum. As the length of the vibrating string is decreased, the pitch of the note gets higher.

How do we change the pitch of the sounds that wind instruments make?

On some wind instruments, such as a trumpet, there are **valves**. Pressing these closes off the column of air inside the instrument at various places. This makes the vibrating column of air longer or shorter. With other instruments, such as the flute or saxophone, the player opens and closes holes along the length of the tube. This has the same effect as making the tube longer or shorter.

EXPERIMENT: How can I make music with drinking-glasses and water?

HYPOTHESIS:
The note made by a glass when struck depends on how full it is.

EQUIPMENT:
A set of six or more glasses, a wooden spoon and water.

EXPERIMENT STEPS:
1 Pour a little water into the first glass, twice as much into the next glass, three times as much into the next and so on.
2 Listen to the notes that the glasses give out when tapped. See if you can play tunes.
3 Try tuning your glasses by comparing them with a musical instrument. Alter the amount of water in each glass until they play notes with the same pitch as the notes on the instrument.
4 Write down which glasses gave a higher sound and which gave a lower sound.

CONCLUSION:
The more water there is in a glass, the lower the pitch of the note it gives out. More water in the glass makes the glass vibrate slower. The lower frequency means the pitch will be lower.

How do I talk?

We have a combined string and wind instrument in our throats. The human voice is made by means of breath from our lungs passing over the **vocal cords** in our throat. The vocal cords are two small pieces of elastic tissue in the larynx, the lump at the front of the throat. Air passing over the vocal cords makes them **vibrate**. Muscles in the larynx can make them tighter to change the **pitch**. This is how we make higher and lower sounds.

Why do we need to change our speaking pitch?

The different **sounds** that make up words are mixtures of high, medium and low sounds. You can see the importance of having all these if you alter the **tone control** on a radio or CD player. For example, you can remove the high-pitched part of the sound by turning down the **treble** control.

Why are voices so different?

This choir has singers with both low and high voices. The vocal cords of men are longer than those of women and children, and so their voices are deeper.

DEMONSTRATION: How speech is produced.

To find out how speech is produced, follow the steps below. All you need is a magazine or a book with some text to read out loud.

DEMONSTRATION STEPS:

1 Keeping the lips still: with your mouth slightly open, but not moving your lips at all, read out a few sentences. Which vowels and consonants sound best, which worst?

2 Keeping the tongue still: press the tip of the tongue against the back of the lower front teeth and keep it there while reading out loud. Press it against the back of the upper front teeth and compare the result.

3 Write down what you heard.

EXPLANATION:
Speech depends not only on the vocal cords but also on all the parts of the mouth working together.

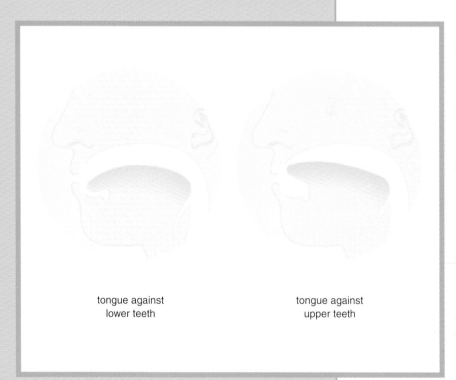

tongue against
lower teeth

tongue against
upper teeth

How do I hear?

We hear **sounds** through our ears. Our ears not only tell us how loud a sound is, and whether it is high- or low-**pitched** – they also tell us approximately where it is coming from.

Suppose a friend standing to your left calls your name. The sound reaches your right ear less than a thousandth of a second later than it reaches the left ear. For the medium- and lower-pitched parts of the sound, the brain can detect this tiny difference in arrival times and turn it into a judgement of which direction your friend is in.

For higher-pitched sounds, the brain uses a different method. The head partly absorbs this sound, so the sound reaching the right ear is less loud. The brain uses the difference in loudness to help work out where the sound is coming from.

What happens inside the ear?

A complicated pathway leads from the outer ear to the brain.
Sound entering the ear strikes a piece of thin tissue called the
eardrum and makes it **vibrate**. These vibrations are passed along
a chain of three small linked bones (the hammer, anvil and stirrup)
to a complicated fluid-filled spiral structure (the cochlea) deeper in
the head. Here tiny hairlike cells are made to vibrate. Finally, nerve
signals (electric currents) travel from the cells to the brain along
the auditory nerve. The brain interprets these as sounds.

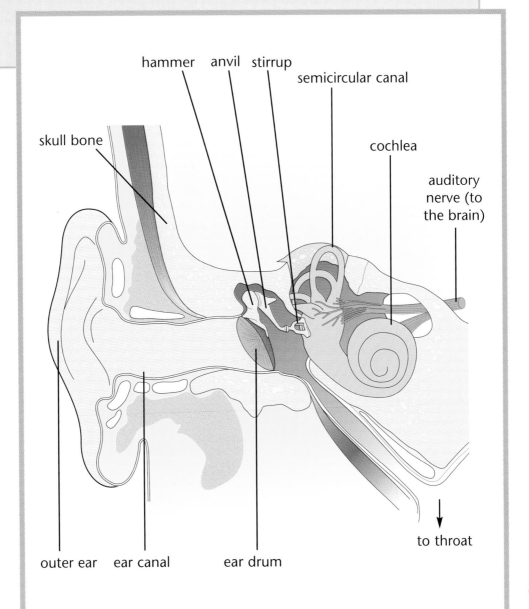

hammer anvil stirrup

semicircular canal

skull bone

cochlea

auditory nerve (to the brain)

to throat

outer ear   ear canal   ear drum

Do animals hear things differently?

Many animals have better **hearing** than we do. Dogs have very sensitive hearing – they often get excited by hearing someone approaching the family house well before their owner can hear anything.

Dogs can also hear higher-pitched sounds than we can. Some dog-owners use **ultrasonic** whistles. These are so high-pitched that human beings cannot hear them.

Elephants can hear low-**frequency** sounds, down to about 5 **hertz**, as compared with the 20 hertz that is the lowest that most human beings can hear.

Why do bats have such big ears?

Bats use sound as a kind of radar. A bat sends out high-pitched squeaks at frequencies as high as 200,000 hertz. These sounds bounce off objects and are picked up by the bat's big, sensitive ears. Bats can avoid obstacles and catch flying insects in the dark thanks to these **echoes**.

INVESTIGATION: Why do we hear sounds differently?

The sound we hear is affected when it passes through matter. You can test this out for yourself by following the steps below. You will need a cassette recorder and tape. Pay careful attention to how your voice sounds in these three different situations:

INVESTIGATION STEPS:

1 Speak a few words out loud in the ordinary way.
2 Repeat, with your hands pressed firmly over both your ears. Does this sound the same or different?
3 **Record** yourself saying the same words, and play back the tape. Does your recorded voice sound the same or different from either of the first two tests?

4 Write down how your voice sounded in each test.

EXPLANATION:

Your voice should have sounded different in each test. In the first test, what you heard consisted partly of sound that had travelled through the air to reach your ears, and partly of sound that had travelled through your head. In the second test, you heard sound that travelled only through your head. In the third test, you heard sound as it reached the **microphone**, after travelling only through the air. This is what other people hear when you speak.

How is sound recorded?

CDs and cassette tapes store **sounds** in the form of a 'picture' of the sound wave. The CD player or tape player translates this 'picture' back into a sound that is a copy of the original.

A CD is a metal disc coated in transparent protective plastic. On one side of the metal there is a spiral 'track', which is a series of tiny pits separated by gaps called 'flats'. The pits and flats are of variable sizes. The pattern of pits and flats is a code representing the loudness and pitch of the sound at each moment. The CD player 'reads' the pattern of pits and flats and turns them into alterations in the strength of an electric current. The current goes from the CD player to **loudspeakers**.

An audio cassette tape consists of a metal-coated plastic tape. The metal is magnetized. The strength of the magnetization varies along the tape, according to the loudness of the sound at the corresponding moment.

INVESTIGATION: How can a sound be sent over a distance?

To demonstrate how we can send speech over a distance, follow the steps below. You will need two empty plastic yoghurt pots and 2 to 3 metres of string.

INVESTIGATION STEPS:

1 Carefully pierce a hole in the bottom of each yoghurt pot and thread one end of the string through. Tie a knot to stop the string sliding out.
2 While a friend holds one pot, you take the other and stretch the string taut between you.
3 Talk, quite quietly, into yours, while your friend holds the other pot to his or her ear. Taking turns, see if you can hold a conversation.

4 Write down what happened.

EXPLANATION:

A taut string can carry a human voice. In the string phone, the **vibrations** in the air caused by your voice make the yoghurt pot vibrate. This in turn makes the string vibrate. The vibrations of the string make the other yoghurt pot vibrate. This sets the air vibrating as sounds that your friend can hear.

People who found the answers

Marin Mersenne (1588 1648)

The pitch of the string is lower for strings that are *longer*, *heavier* or stretched *less tightly*. A French scientist and monk, Marin Mersenne, summed this up in three laws named after him. He counted the vibrations of very long, very slowly vibrating strings and used his laws to calculate how fast the strings of musical instruments vibrate.

Mersenne also made a fairly accurate measurement of the speed of **sound**, by measuring the time required for an **echo** to return when sound was reflected from an obstacle at a known distance.

Thomas Alva Edison (1847–1931)

Our modern world is dominated by moving pictures, recorded sound, telephones and electric power. All of these things were either invented or improved by Edison.

He was a telegraph operator and invented several improvements, such as a printing telegraph, which made a printed **record** of each message.

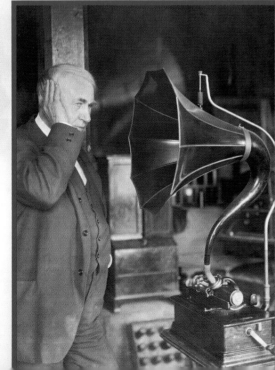

Edison became a full-time inventor and set up his own laboratory. He invented the sort of telephone microphone that is still used, improving the sound of Alexander Graham Bell's newly invented telephone.

In 1877 Edison invented the first 'phonograph', for recording and replaying sound. Later he made the first 'talking pictures', by linking a phonograph with a film projector.

Amazing facts

- During the Second World War, enemy aircraft were detected at a distance by arrays of giant mechanical 'ears'. They consisted of large dishes that collected the faint **sounds** of enemy aircaft and focused them onto **microphones** (see below).

- The loudest sound ever heard was the explosion of the volcano of Krakatoa in 1883. This uninhabited island in the Pacific blew up, raising a wave that drowned 36,000 people on other islands. The sound was loud enough to be heard in Australia, 3000 kilometres away.

- **Ultrasound** is beamed into trees to discover disease deep within the trunk. The sound waves are affected differently by empty spaces in the wood, by unhealthy parts and by parts that have rotted away.

- Hundreds of species of fish make sounds. Some make sounds using their swim-bladder. This is a gas-filled bag in the fish's body that controls how buoyant the fish is. For example, cusk eels drum on the swim-bladder with a special bone. Dolphins and whales locate prey and each other by sending out clicks from the front of their heads.

amplitude strength of a wave. The amplitude of a sound wave is how fast the molecules of air vibrate backwards and forwards. The bigger the amplitude, the louder the sound.

atom one of the small particles that matter is made of. An atom is made of smaller particles, including electrons.

disturbance movement or other alteration of something that was at rest. A sound wave is a disturbance of the air. It consists of vibrations of the particles of the air.

echo sound that bounces off something before reaching a listener. The sound that travels directly reaches the listener first, because it has less far to go – then the echo is heard.

frequency how often something repeats in a second. The frequency of a sound is the number of sound waves that pass in one second.

hearing ability of animals and human beings to detect sound

hertz basic unit of frequency, symbol Hz. A sound has a frequency of 200 Hz, for example, if 200 waves pass a particular point every second.

loudspeaker device that produces sound using the electric current from a radio, CD player, TV set or other such device

microphone device that detects sounds for recording, amplifying or broadcasting

molecule group of atoms linked together. The atoms in most of the matter around us are in the form of molecules, rather than being single atoms.

music sounds made by human beings and arranged to be pleasing or exciting

noise any sound, but especially one that is not wanted because it is loud, unpleasant or out of place

note single musical sound with a definite pitch

pitch how high or low a sound is. The pitch is high if high frequencies are strongest in the sound, and low if low frequencies are strongest.

record/recording pattern of magnetism on a magnetic tape, or of pits in a plastic disc (CD), which is a 'picture' of sound. The recording can be used to produce sound that is a copy of the original.

siren device that makes a very loud warning sound. Sirens are mounted on emergency vehicles to warn other traffic to clear the way.

sonar method of using sound to detect objects under water. A sonar device on a ship or submarine sends out sound waves that are reflected by objects such as the sea floor, shoals of fish, or other submarines. A computer in the sonar device turns the echoes into a picture of the surroundings.

sound waves consisting of vibrations of molecules, that travel through air, water or solid materials. Human beings can hear those that are not too high or too low in frequency.

tone control control on a radio set, tape player, CD player or other sound system that alters the amount of high- or low-frequency sound

treble high-pitched part of a sound, especially music or the sound from a radio, CD player and so on

ultrasonic sound of a very high frequency, 20,000 hertz and above

valve on a musical wind instrument, a device that when pressed alters the length of the tubing that the air is blown through. This lets the player produce a different range of notes.

vibrate/vibration rapid backwards-and-forwards motion. Sound waves consist of vibrations of molecules of air, water or whatever material the sound is passing through.

vocal cords two pieces of elastic tissue in the larynx, which is the lump at the front of the throat. The vocal cords vibrate when air from the lungs passes over them, producing many of the sounds of speech.

wavelength distance from one crest of a wave to the next. In the case of a sound wave, a 'crest' is a place where the vibrating molecules are moving fastest, either forwards or backwards.

► Index

► More books to read

Fascinating Science Projects: Sound, Bobbi Searle
   (Franklin Watts, 2002)
Science Fact Files: Light and Sound, Steve Parker
   (Hodder Wayland, 2001)
Exploring Science: Exploring Electricity, Ed Catherall
   (Hodder Wayland, 1990)
Science Scene Topic Books: Sound and Music, Jane Cartledge
   and John Avison (Hodder & Stoughton Educational, 1993)